The Cartoon Bleu Cookbook

Living and Cooking in Île de France

Yvonne van Roekel

Illustrated by
Peter Bellchambers

Book design: Korongo Books
ISBN: 978-1-943741-09-0

About the Author

Yvonne van Roekel was born below sea level but managed to crawl up the nearest sand dune and gaze at the sunsets over the North Sea Canal, watching the ships sailing off to mysterious worlds. They inspired her to travel and to live in Oregon, Norway, Hong Kong, Singapore, California, Portugal, and France. A former food critic and contributing editor to the *Algarve Magazine*, she has never been able to kick the writing habit.

CONTENTS

Introduction

You are leafing through this book in your favorite bookshop and you wonder what this book is all about.

It is about our corner of France, about trees that die and friendships that live. Neighbors who are friends and villagers who become friends.

This book is about embracing life: people, dogs, pheasants, ducks, and the odd necromancer.

It is about food and fun and "Babette's Feast."

It describes life in France. It does not describe life from France.

Our France is situated sixty kilometers south of Paris and suitably (perspectively speaking) close to northern Europe's escape routes to the sun.

All year long we are called on by relations, friends, and the occasional scrounging, uninvited visitor: "Just a day's drive! How absolutely splendid of you to live here." They always arrive at dinnertime. In addition to the habitual trans-European migratory guests, we are frequently visited by friendly villagers, who call, for example, to bring young lettuce plants for the kitchen garden. They come to ask advice on an English translation, and they come to give advice on when to plant garlic, or on how to prepare wild mushrooms gathered from our forests—the same forests that enraptured the landscape painters of the Barbizon School. This is the France you will discover in *The Cartoon Bleu Cookbook*.

I wrote this book for you and your loved ones. I wrote it for people who love to cook for people (and their dogs). People who are charmed by France, by new and exciting recipes, and by gentle humor. The recipes attempt to inspire, using herbs and local produce and, in case you have the luxury of a kitchen garden, creating dishes with produce that is fresh and untreated. Some of the spices and ingredients come from Asia; I lived in Singapore for many years and I have never been able to kick the habit. I can only hope that you enjoy them as much as I do. Love, after all, is the most important ingredient, in cooking as in life.

—*Yvonne van Roekel and Peter Bellchambers*

Madame de Surgères

Madame de Surgères glanced at her watch and sighed. "I suppose it's time for me to go back to my prison. The gates shut at nine o'clock."

She took a last sip of her coffee, fumbled for her walking stick, and slowly shuffled into our courtyard.

"Thank you, my young friends. Dining with people who are not anesthetized by television is such a relief for me." She looked wistfully at our house and waved at it with her stick.

"The house? You are still happy with her? She doesn't give you many problems?"

The house had caught our attention five weeks previously, when we spotted an aerial photograph in an estate agent's window. It popped out from a pine-covered, sun-drenched hill, bewitching us the moment we stepped inside. Ignoring our architectural backgrounds, we decided that instant we would buy.

"Don't you trust me," purred the house. "I have been standing here long before your parents were born."

At this first visit to Lastenfurst House, the eighty-two-year-old owner shook our hands firmly, but halfway through our "*Enchanté*," she waved her hand impatiently and snapped, "Yes, yes. Do you know anything about gardening or keeping up a property?"

The estate agent, who until then had seemed a very kindly and patient man of retirement age, rolled his eyes.

"Madame de Surgères, I did explain over the phone that Madame is an interior architect and Monsieur a landscape architect. Surely—"

"That may be so, young man, but drawing pretty plans doesn't guarantee that Monsieur and Madame know anything at all about practical matters."

I suppressed a smile and wandered over to admire one of the many paintings that crowded the walls. It was a portrait of a man painted by an artist who must have loved him. The brushstrokes revealed tenderness and an intimacy with the subject.

"My godmother was an artist. That is my godfather. Do you like it?"

I admitted that I did and in halting French explained why. Madame de Surgères looked sternly at the estate agent and said accusingly, "Monsieur Chaigneau, you told me Madame was English. I do not distinguish an English accent." Turning to me, she added, "You sound Scandinavian."

"I am Dutch."

"Good. At least the Dutch are clean. Like the Austrians. I am Austrian by birth."

My French was still at beginner's level, so I continued our conversation in German, and Madame de Surgères broke out in her first smile. When we left half an hour later, she gave us a large bouquet of lilacs from her garden, with the invitation to visit her whenever we liked.

"This was the nicest I have ever seen her," said Monsieur Chaigneau. "But I must warn you. Four times I have had clients who wanted to buy the house, and each time we sat down to sign the contract with the old battle-ax, she changed her mind at the last minute and refused to sign."

Two weeks later, when we too sat down to sign the contract, our estate agent was visibly tense. He shifted nervously in his chair, cleared his throat and handed her the papers and a pen.

"You are sure? You love this house? You will take care of my garden?" Madame de Surgères looked at me pleadingly. As she blinked away a tear, she visibly shrank and looked much less formidable.

"If only my knees had not given up, I could have kept her a little longer. Now I am condemned to share my life with some old geriatrics who have nothing better to do with their lives than watch television while waiting to die."

Monsieur Chaigneau coughed and rearranged the papers. The "old battle-ax" took over once more. Grabbing the pen from his hand, she said irritably, "Don't worry, you'll get your commission. Please allow me the importance of this moment."

She turned to me and asked in German, "Why, of all the houses you have seen, did you choose this one?"

I had asked myself the same question and could only think of one reason:

"The house chose us."

She nodded her head in agreement, as if this was a most logical explanation, then picked up the pen and signed the contract.

Madame de Surgères remained in the house for another month before moving to a nearby retirement home, and during that time I visited often, both to see her and to measure the house so I could draw up the plans for the renovation. We often had long conversations over a cup of coffee and a generous slice of her rich and wonderful Austrian tortes. Over that month I came to know the life story of a remarkable woman. She was born Aloisa Weissbacker in a small village near Innsbrück at the beginning of the last century. Her mother had died when she was seven years old, and very soon after that—too soon for the grieving Aloisa—her father had remarried. His daughter could not and would not accept his new wife, and she refused to speak to her father from the moment he brought his young bride into the house.

When, after one year of domestic silence, her French godparents came to visit, Aloisa begged them to take her with them. The couple was childless and adored their godchild, so with everyone's consent the young girl moved to France.

When Aloisa turned fifteen, she decided that she was going to marry a friend of the family, Jacques de Surgères, thirty years her senior and a confirmed bachelor. Jacques was at first amused by the strong-willed Austrian, but over the next few years he came to love her. He proposed marriage when she turned eighteen. Since Aloisa had never been legally adopted by her godparents, she still needed her father's permission to marry. He flatly refused.

"You never approved of my marriage. I'm returning you the favor."

Jacques and Aloisa had to wait until she turned twenty-one.

It was a happy marriage that was to last eighteen years. Jacques encouraged his wife to study at the Sorbonne; he taught her to play golf and to drive a car. He took her to Russia, Asia, and the Middle East. A few months before the Second World War broke out, Jacques was sent on a contract to Boston, where they stayed until the end of the war. They returned to France in 1946, where Jacques fell ill. He died a few months later.

"My life was finished," Madame de Surgères told me, "so I decided to give the rest of it to God. I only prayed He wouldn't need me for too long and would let me join my Jacques."

At the age of forty she entered a convent and was sent to Norway to teach French, but when her godmother died in 1960, she left her beloved convent to come back to France, where she devoted herself to the care of her invalid godfather. When he too passed away ten years later, she inherited the house and turned her devotion toward God and garden.

"Now I have such trouble walking, I am no longer able to take care of the place. Rather than let it deteriorate, I decided to sell the house, but only to someone who would love it as much as I did."

Madame de Surgères did not visit us until after the renovation was finished. One glorious autumn day she came zipping up our drive and parked her new little red car expertly next to ours.

"Thank God I can still drive. Otherwise I would go mad in that lunatic asylum."

I helped her out of the car, and she squeezed my arm affectionately. When I offered her a drink, she shook her head.

"No time for that, I came to see the renovations. Now show me."

I was a little nervous as I took her arm and led her through the house, but I needn't have worried.

"This has always been my dream. To break through all these confining walls. My godmother would have approved. The quality of light is wonderful."

She refused a second offer of a drink.

"No time. Lunch is served at twelve sharp, and the food is the only thing worthwhile in Purgatory."

As she backed out of our drive, a delivery van came racing down the street and only just managed to avoid her. The driver stopped his car and got out. Still shaking with nerves, he yelled, "You stupid old woman. I could have killed you."

Madame de Surgères calmly rolled down her window.

"You would have done me a favor. I have been waiting to join my husband for forty-six years."

She waved for the driver to move out of the way and drove off.

A few months later Madame de Surgères unexpectedly arrived

at the house. "I'm not staying," she announced. "I only came to say goodbye. I'm off to Austria for a month's visit. I am eighty-five now, and maybe soon the good God will show his mercy and let me join my Jacques. It's time to apologize to my half-brother for not accepting his mother."

I offered to take her to the airport, but she said, "Why should I go by plane? I would have no transport once I'm there. No, no, I'm driving."

"Alone?"

"I can't stand driving with someone chattering beside me. I like to drive alone."

When she came back, she reported that the trip had been a success. Her only problem had been getting in and out of her car, because her crutches would get in the way.

"But God always sent someone to help me."

Madame de Surgères continued to visit us and sometimes she would allow herself to stay for dinner. She had been a creative cook in her day and loved to discuss recipes with me. Supporting her chin with her hands folded over one of her crutches, she would sit on a kitchen chair and comment on my preparation of the dinner.

"Pork and apples. Cream and calvados. The very soul of Normandy. Wait, you have added sage. I love the smell of sage. Jacques used to love sage."

That evening we were in a creative mood and devised a recipe for pancakes using potatoes and celeriac. Madame de Surgères inhaled through her nose when I dropped the batter in the goose fat.

"That smells wonderful. I do like the combination of potatoes and celeriac. Have you ever tried celeriac just by itself? I used to cut the root into matchsticks on a mandoline. I would sprinkle them with lemon juice. It keeps them white, you know, and it adds flavor. Jacques liked these celeriac sticks fried in a little bit of goose fat with a few caraway seeds and some parsley. *Wunderschön* with duck!"

Later, over coffee after our dinner, Madame de Surgères was explaining how to make a linzer torte. She stopped mid-sentence and stated out of the blue, "I'm sick and tired of the rules and regulations in that retirement prison. A few months ago I applied for a small independent bungalow within a large retirement complex in the Loire. The grounds are beautifully landscaped and each bungalow has its own small garden. Yesterday they sent me confirmation that there will be one available in December. I'll be free, dear friends. I'll be free. However, tonight . . ."

When she left, she rolled down the window of her car and announced, "Tomorrow I am going to Norway. I want to see my old friends in the convent one last time. I will come and visit you on my way back."

"You're driving?"

"Alone," she confirmed.

Normandy Pork Fillet

Serves 4 to 6

- *1.5 pounds (750 grams) pork fillet*
- *A few sprigs of sage, plus more for garnish*
- *1 large garlic clove*
- *1/4 cup apple juice*
- *1/2 teaspoon sea salt, or to taste*
- *1 tablespoon butter*
- *1 measure of calvados*
- *1 small onion, sliced in thin rings*
- *2 small green apples, coarsely chopped*
- *1/2 cup crème fraîche*
- *Freshly ground pepper*

In a food processor, blend the sage, garlic, apple juice, and salt until smooth. Marinate the pork in the mixture for at least 4 hours and preferably overnight, turning the meat several times.

Remove the fillet from the marinade and wipe dry with a paper towel. Heat the butter in a frying pan and quickly sear the meat on both sides. Warm the calvados, pour it over the meat, and flambé, shaking the pan until the flames die down. Lower the heat, add the marinade, and simmer for 30 minutes on low heat. Add the chopped apple and sliced onion and cook another 10 minutes or until done. Remove the fillet from the pan and keep it warm. Add the crème fraîche to the apple mixture and simmer for another 2 minutes. At the same time, slice the fillet and return it to the pan for 1 minute. Give a generous twist with the pepper mill and serve with the sauce on top. Garnish with a sprig of fresh sage.

Potato and Celeriac Pancakes

Serves 4 to 6

- 12 ounces (300 grams) potatoes
- 10 ounces (250 grams) celeriac
- 1 tablespoon finely chopped fresh sage, plus more for garnish
- 2 garlic cloves
- 1 tablespoon heavy cream
- 1 large egg
- 2 tablespoons rice flour
- 2 ounces (50 grams) grated fresh Parmesan cheese
- Freshly ground salt and pepper
- 3 tablespoons goose or duck fat

Peel and grate the potatoes. Put them in a colander lined with cheesecloth and place a heavy weight on top. Leave for one hour to expel the moisture.

Blend the sage, garlic, and cream in a food processor. Whisk the egg and fold into the cream mixture.

Peel and grate the celeriac, and immediately mix all ingredients except the goose fat in a bowl. Season to taste.

Heat the fat in a nonstick pan or cast-iron griddle until very hot. Drop the pancake mixture one spoonful at a time into the hot fat, and flatten it with a spatula. Fry until golden crisp on both sides.

Serve with some of the chopped sage.

Linzer Torte

Makes 12 slices

- *1 cup unbleached flour*
- *1 teaspoon baking powder*
- *2 sticks (3/4 cup) butter*
- *1/2 cup brown sugar*
- *1/2 cup chopped hazelnuts*
- *1 teaspoon cinnamon*
- *1/2 teaspoon nutmeg*
- *2 teaspoons cocoa powder*
- *1 egg yolk*
- *1 measure kirsch*
- *1 jar raspberry jam*

Sift together the flour and the baking powder. Add all the ingredients except the jam, one by one. Knead until all the ingredients are well incorporated. Refrigerate for 2 hours.

Roll out 2/3 of the dough and line a well-buttered pie pan with the dough. Spread the jam evenly over the dough. Cut the remaining dough in strips and arrange over the jam in a diamond pattern. Bake for 40 minutes at 350 degrees F. (180 degrees C.).

Store, covered, and in a dark cool place for a few days to improve the taste.

Tree Troubles 1

One by one, the Scots pines on our south-facing hill are dying. Some have come down in wet winter storms, while others hold out until felled by nature's whim or by human design. Their fate caught our attention one dreary autumn, when a large group of the evergreen trees started dropping their needles in what appeared to be a solidarity pact with the giant oak tree that shades part of our garden in summer.

Alarmed, I phoned the prefecture of our department for advice.

"You will have to get in touch with the agricultural department," whined the *serveur vocal* from the information department.

"Call the environment department," barked an impatient civil servant at the agricultural department. He slammed down the phone before I had a chance to ask for the number. Glancing at my watch I understood the error of my ways. One cannot expect co-operation from a government official five minutes before lunchtime.

"Dead trees are not our concern," tittered a merry environment officer after his liquid lunch. "I advise you to call the forestry service."

Determined to unravel the knot of red tape, I doggedly dialed the forestry department's number.

"We'll send an expert as soon as one is free," pledged the *ingénieur* who answered the phone at the forestry department. He insisted the visit would be scheduled within the next few days, but I decided not to hold my breath.

The very next morning a tattered little Deux Chevaux pulled

into our drive. A bouncy Labrador bolted over the driver, through the opening door, and up into the garden.

"Laurent Fernier, forestry department," acknowledged the lanky young *ingénieur* as he disentangled himself from the car. Straightening his crumpled Barbour jacket, he shook my hand firmly, then turned to call his dog.

"Here, Einstein!" The Labrador boomeranged down the hill and was ordered to sit. He wagged his tail furiously, jumped up to lick my face, and then spun around to give his full attention to three magpies squawking in the chestnut tree overhead.

"I am partial to contradictions, " explained Fernier with a bright smile when I questioned the suitability of his dog's name.

"Are you also partial to coffee and apple pie?" I proposed in an effort to make up for my Dutch directness. He eagerly admitted that he was and then turned to investigate the dying pines.

Twenty minutes later Fernier, Einstein at his feet, sat at the kitchen table with a cup of coffee, carrying on excitedly about the recent drought, *Stenographes*, *Regium*, *Sirex* and other *ravageurs*. I tried to follow his discourse, but he had completely lost me after the *Stenographe*, largely because he had placed a squirmy specimen on the table as evidence, and it was now maggoting its way toward the apple pie. Thankfully he intercepted the wandering worm, replaced it into the sample bag, and tucked into the pie.

"This is very good," he complimented between mouthfuls. "Would you be upset if I asked you for the recipe?"

I told him I did not have an exact recipe, since that morning's apple pie had developed from a basic recipe, to which I had added ingredients according to inspiration and availability.

"No problem, you tell me what you did, and I'll write it down," Fernier suggested cheerfully as he devoured another piece of pie.

After a few minutes and many oh-I-forgots, we had managed to reconstruct the recipe. Fernier got up to leave, shaking my hand and gently nudging awake the sleeping Einstein. As he reversed out onto the road, he waved the recipe out of the car window and shouted, "Thank you for this and the coffee. I'll have the samples analyzed in the laboratory. You should receive the official report in a few days."

Two days later the report arrived, together with a neatly typed recipe titled "Einstein's Apple Pie."

Einstein's Apple Pie

For the crust:
- *8 ounces (250 grams) self-raising flour*
- *5 ounces (150 gram) granulated brown sugar*
- *1/4 cup chopped hazelnuts*
- *1/2 teaspoon cinnamon*
- *Pinch of salt*
- *Grated rind of half a lemon*
- *6 ounces (175 grams) butter*
- *5 tablespoons dry cider, chilled*

For the filling:
- *1/2 cup crème fraîche*
- *5 tablespoons brown sugar, or to taste*
- *1 egg, lightly beaten*
- *1 tablespoon corn flour (maizena)*
- *1 measure of calvados*
- *1/2 teaspoon cinnamon*
- *3 to 4 tart apples, chopped*
- *4 to 5 tablespoons raisins*
- *1/3 cup chopped hazelnuts*

To make the crust: Mix the flour, sugar, chopped hazelnuts, cinnamon, salt, and grated lemon rind in a bowl. Cut in the butter with a fork until the dough becomes grainy. Add the cider and work into the dough just enough so it forms a ball. Wrap and let it rest in the refrigerator for 1 hour. Line a 26-centimeter buttered pie pan with the dough and trim the overhang. Form balls the size of marbles with the leftover pastry.

Preheat the oven to 190 degrees C.

To make the filling: Whisk together all ingredients except the apples, raisins, and hazelnuts until totally incorporated. Drop in the chopped apples and the raisins; toss well to coat. Spoon the mixture into the pastry-lined pan.

Top with the hazelnuts and the balls of pastry and bake for 50 to 60 minutes. Serve topped with cream.

Tree Troubles 2

What do they know?" scoffed our next-door neighbor, Alex, after I had shown him the laboratory's report. "Tell me, who is the expert? Some guy in his white coat, gawking through a microscope, or my father, who has been a forester for more than thirty years? Papa knows these trees. According to him the Scots pine in this area have been dying since the early seventies, long before there were any droughts."

Alex is a man of small stature and large opinions, a benevolent Buddha disguised as an aging Hell's Angel, who wears a golden earring and a pigtail to keep up with the times.

"Anyway, the only piece of intelligent advice I can read in this exposé is that there is nothing to be done, except to take them down."

He held the paper out in front of him, and pretending to adjust an imaginary pair of reading glasses, he began to quote from the report in a magisterial voice:

"We therefore recommend you remove, foremost, and at your earliest convenience, the Pinus sylvestris specimens which form a direct threat to your domicile. Only licensed foresters should be contracted." At this, he threw his arms across his rotund torso and let out a belly laugh.

"Licensed foresters, hah," he snorted. "Two or three strong guys, a pulley, and some chains, that's all we need. I'll organize it for next Sunday, and don't worry, I'll ask Papa to come and supervise." Glancing at the one tree that was leaning precariously toward our house, he added, "That one is the first to go. We don't want Pinus sylvestris to damage your illustrious domicile."

The next Sunday Alex came around to tell us that he had organized the strong men and the chains but, unfortunately, had not been able to get hold of a pulley. Since we would not be able to cut down any trees, he suggested we come over for lunch and get to know the work team.

The week after that he had tracked down the pulley, but this time the work team could not be organized and we would have to wait until the following Sunday.

When the men went to the shed to get the tools on that day, they found a note where the pulley and chains should have been:

"Alex, I came to borrow your chains and you weren't in. I'll return them next week. See you then, André."

So it continued for the next few months. Something or someone always prevented the hazardous tree from being felled. There were two or three Sundays where all the necessary elements were actually available, but our gregarious neighbor would insist that the team should have lunch first to fortify themselves for the heavy task at hand. These lunches had the habit of taking up most of the afternoons with animated discussions, sustained by numerous bottles of Burgundy. When eventually the decision was made to go out and remove the tree, it would be either too dark or I would vote against the effort when some of the team members had delighted in too many *digestifs*.

One windy Sunday morning I was preparing a lentil soup when Alex popped his head around the kitchen door.

"Today is the day, dear neighbor. Today we shall remove the offending tree."

As luck would have it, Peter was out and would not be back before three o'clock.

"Not to worry. Leave a note for him, bring whatever you're brewing in that magical red pot of yours, and come and have lunch with us. We'll do the job as soon as Peter comes back."

Peter came in at three, informing us that the wind had picked up quite considerably and that the job would have to be done soon, before a real storm would develop. He protested insincerely when

Alex poured him a glass of wine and disappeared into the kitchen to fetch him a bowl of steaming hot lentil soup.

Three glasses of wine and a cheese board later, the old trusted and tried debate "Globalization, yes or no?" was dusted off once more and in full swing. The afternoon faded into shades of evening, when Alex brought out his father's finest bottle of home-brewed marc. The valiant resolution to fell the tree was in danger of being postponed yet again, so I suggested we should drink the marc in celebration of successfully carrying out the task at hand. The team and Peter scrambled hastily to their feet, collected their tools, and marched off into our garden.

They had not been longer than a few minutes, when all four of them piled back into the dining room.

"Already done?" I asked in amazement.

"Already done! Can we have that glass of marc?"

They were suspiciously quiet as Alex poured out five glasses, so I ventured to ask how they had managed to do such a laborious chore in such a short time.

They sipped their drinks in uneasy silence.

"All right, what happened with the tree?" I demanded to know.

The four friends looked at each other to find a suitable spokesman, but before any of them could volunteer, I raced outside toward our house.

There was the tree, uprooted and firmly embedded into our garage roof. It had bounced off the main house, leaving a gaping hole in the roof, and on it's way down it had ripped off the rain gutter as well.

"It wasn't our fault," Alex said when he caught up with me. "We never touched it. The storm took it down while we were having lunch, but don't worry, we'll repair the damage next Sunday."

Lentil Soup
Serves 6 to 8

- 4 ounces (100 grams) diced bacon
- 1 tablespoon chopped rosemary
- 2 medium onions, chopped
- 4 garlic cloves, minced
- 1 carrot, thinly sliced
- Pinch ground cumin
- 4 pints (2 liters) beef stock
- 1 bay leaf
- 5 juniper berries, bruised
- 5 whole black peppercorns
- 1 large can of brown lentils
- 1 cup sour cream or yogurt
- Pinch cayenne pepper
- 4 dry, spicy garlic sausages, sliced
- Sour cream for garnish

In a heavy soup pan, fry the bacon and rosemary until crisp. Remove and set aside. In the released fat, fry the onions, garlic, and carrot until soft. Add the cumin. Add the broth and spices and simmer for 30 minutes. Strain and reserve the cooked vegetables. Remove the bay leaf and berries.

In a food processor, blend the cooked vegetables, one cup of the stock, the lentils, sour cream, and cayenne pepper. Add to remaining stock and stir in the bacon and sausage. Warm through and serve with an extra dollop of sour cream. Serve a good sourdough bread and a salad as accompaniments.

Chicory and Apple Salad
Serves 6 to 8

For the dressing:
- *2 tablespoons walnut oil*
- *3 tablespoons safflower oil*
- *2 tablespoons sherry vinegar*
- *1 teaspoon honey*
- *1 teaspoon mustard*
- *Salt to taste*

Last touch:
- *6 heads of chicory*
- *2 tart apples, peeled and diced*
- *2 tablespoons raisins*
- *2 tablespoons pine nuts*
- *1 tablespoon chopped chives*

Combine all ingredients for the dressing in a processor and blend until smooth. Remove the bitter stem from the chicory and cut into bite-size pieces. Add the apples, raisins, and pine nuts, and mix with the dressing. Sprinkle the chives on top.

Hound-Duck

Monsieur Boudet is our oil supplier. Twice a year he pulls up in front of our house in his SHELL tanker-truck and conversely delivers two thousand liters of BP diesel, which our central heating and hot water boiler gulp greedily with ever increasing thirst. I once chided him about this disparity between his brand supply and its publicity. He muttered something in the style of "oil moves in mysterious ways," avoiding eye contact, and gushed in the same breath that I should put some anti-freeze in the tank. He filled our tank without another word and then was gone. Since our conversation was taking place in early May, I deduced that I had stumbled upon a second taboo subject in France. Never question a person's political party preference and never question his oil company loyalty.

On other delivery days, though, Monsieur Boudet enjoys engaging me in a tarrying debate. With one conscientious eye on our oil tank and the other eye bright and blue on me, he will defend, for example, why hunters such as he are in fact preserving nature's bounty, rather than destroying it. In this particular dispute I showed him my collection of spent cartridges and empty packets of Gauloises that I had harvested from country lanes during the previous hunting season.

"Parisians!" he scoffed. "Race in their four-wheel drives to the country all dressed up like Rambo. Ten of them shooting at the same tame pheasant."

He acted out his version of this dastardly deed in our drive, reeling back in mock recoil from the clumsy shot.
"It is the damn Parisians, I tell you."

With this verdict he climbed back into his truck, but not before collecting the check and his small son, whom he had brought along for the ride. You see, Monsieur Boudet does not like riding alone. On delivery days our sociable supplier brings along either a friend, one of his children, his dog, or even, at times, his cat to keep him company.

One year, on a dripping and misty morning in November, he climbed down from his truck unaccompanied. I was just about to ask him why he had been so cruelly abandoned, when from out of his cabin slipped a sound much like the garrulous quacking of a duck. I asked, "What's that noise in your truck?"

Boudet flashed a mischievous smile.

"I have the pleasure of introducing you to Judas." He opened the cabin door reverently. A very indignant duck hopped from the passenger's seat onto his shoulder and willfully pecked at his neck in rebuke for being kept prisoner inside the truck.

Catching my look of amused bewilderment he continued: "Four months ago this duck waddled from the stream bordering my garden onto our patio and demanded to be fed. Much to my surprise, Chico, our spaniel, sniffed at the bird, wagged his tail, and gently pushed the duck toward his food bowl. Next thing I know, there they were all cuddled up together in the dog's basket, and they have been friends ever since." I was not sure whether to believe his unlikely story, but the mallard was definitely behaving like a pet. If it was not the truth, it was still a damn good story, so I said, "I am curious. Why have you named him Judas?"

Boudet moved his oil-stained cap to the back of his head, scratched his brow, then burst out laughing.

"Would you believe, Madame, that on the first day of the hunt, this duck would not let us get into the car without him? Chico raced around my Renault in eager anticipation, and this jealous bird wanted to share in the fun. He created such a fuss that I decided to take him along with us. Well, Chico spent most of that day protecting his friend from the other dogs on the hunt. When I finally, toward the end of the afternoon, managed to shoot a wild duck, I felt extremely guilty.

"In the event, I needn't have worried because when Chico put the bird at my feet, this traitor here gave the dog an affection- ate peck. He then flapped onto my shoulder, scanned the sky and quacked as if to say, 'Well done. Now let's get some more.' And that is why I have called him Judas."

I smiled suspiciously on hearing this explanation.

"Ah, Madame does not believe me?" Monsieur Boudet retorted. "Here, look at this." From his wallet he produced a clipping from our local newspaper. It was an article about this extraordinary duck, accompanied by a picture of Boudet with his hunting friends, Judas on his shoulder and Chico at his feet. I had to admit that this piece of evidence proved conclusive.

When the two of them prepared to leave, Boudet turned to me and said, "Oh, by the way. My wife thanks you for that trout recipe you gave her last time. Do you, by chance, have any new recipes for duck?"

Duck Salad With Kumquat and Hazelnut Dressing

Serves 4 to 6

For the dressing:
- 1/2 cup hazelnuts
- 1 tablespoon ginger-flavored rice wine (or 1 teaspoon finely minced ginger and 1 tablespoon dry sherry)
- 1 teaspoon soy sauce
- 1/2 tablespoon raspberry vinegar
- 1 tablespoon grain-style mustard
- 2 tablespoons kumquat sauce (or 2 tablespoons orange marmalade)

For the duck:
- 16 ounces (400 grams) duck breast, sliced thinly and cut into 25-millimeter strips
- 1/2 teaspoon five-spice powder (or 1/4 teaspoon each of cinnamon and all-spice)
- Salt to taste
- 1 tablespoon butter

Last touch:
- Medium oak-leaf lettuce
- Small bunch chives, finely chopped
- Borage or nasturtium flowers to decorate (optional)

Note: Ginger-flavored rice wine, kumquat sauce, and five-spice powder are available at Chinese markets

Put all the ingredients for the dressing in a blender and blend until the dressing has a crunchy consistency.

Season the duck with the five-spice powder and salt. Sauté the duck strips in the butter for 3 minutes. Reserve and keep warm.

Wash, dry, and shred the lettuce into bite-size pieces. Stir the dressing into the warm duck pieces and arrange over the lettuce. Sprinkle generously with the chives and decorate with the flowers.

Tagliatelli With Basil
Serves 4 to 6

- *1 bunch of spring onions, diced*
- *1 cup of mushrooms, sliced*
- *3 cloves garlic, minced*
- *2 tablespoons grapeseed oil*
- *1/2 cup crème fraîche*
- *4 tablespoons grated Parmesan*
- *1 bunch of basil, chopped*
- *16 ounces (400 grams) fresh tagliatelli*
- *Freshly ground black pepper*
- *Basil leaves for garnish*

Fry the spring onions, mushrooms, and garlic in the oil until soft. Add the crème fraîche, cheese, and basil. Warm through for 1 minute.

Cook the pasta for 3 minutes in salted, boiling water, drain, and rinse under cold water.

Mix with the mushroom sauce, warm through, and add freshly ground pepper in generous amounts.

Decorate with a few basil leaves.

Katya

I am sorry to interrupt, but . . ."
Our neighbor Michelle hovered near our kitchen door, dressed in a faded pink peignoir.

". . . you're the local linguists, so Joseph and I thought you might be able to help this young woman."

In the darkness I discerned the silhouette of an athletic-looking girl who was standing timidly a few steps behind Michelle.

"You know, she knocked on our door a few minutes ago and started gabbling, but she doesn't speak one word of French."

The damsel in question let out a tiny sob, and the reflection of the street lamp caught a rolling tear.

"She is clearly upset, but we don't know why. Can't you try out some of your languages on her?"

Obligingly, I began to cross-examine the young woman alphabetically beginning with "Do you speak English?" Each question met with a dejected shake of the head. Finally, after "A senhora è Portuguesa?" she slumped her shoulders in defeat and whimpered, "Njet, njet."

"By God, she is Russian," whooped Peter.

" Da, da, Rrhoose," confirmed the girl.

"Joseph, she is Russian," shouted Michelle to her husband, who was guarding his front door, suspecting a setup.

Remembering friends in Paris who speak Russian, Peter told Michelle to go home and not to worry. We would let the young lady speak on the phone with our friends in order to find out why she needed our help. I noticed a small skip of relief as Michelle turned to cross the road after this fortuitous release from reluctant responsibility.

Back in the warmth of our living room we soon discovered that our protégé's name was Katya. However, she had no papers, no money, nor any piece of identification on her. To complicate matters, a babysitter answered the phone at our Russian-speaking friends' apartment and told us that Mr. and Mrs. Klimoff were at a cocktail party. It had turned eight o'clock, and we were hungry. After pointing alternatively to my stomach, my mouth, and our unexpected guest, Katya indicated that she was hungry as well. A thorough search amid the leftovers from the previous week (our planned dinner), yielded a tub with fresh chicken livers, a few spring onions, two leeks, a block of tofu, and some mushrooms. I prayed Katya would like Chinese food.

While I prepared the meal, Peter tried to reach the Klimoffs again, and Katya watched me in the kitchen, chirping, "Da, da," each time I reached for a new ingredient.

During the dinner we finally thought of using drawings to find out where Katya might belong. She had either come by train or was staying at a friend's house near a railway, had gone for a solitary walk in the forest, and after climbing to the top of a hill, she had lost her bearings on the way down. Wandering through the forest quite lost, she eventually reached a road in total darkness and decided to ring at the first house. Katya closed her eyes and shivered to indicate she had been very scared. We resolved that after dinner Peter would drive with her to Buno railway station and start the search for her friend's house from there.

As they walked out of the back door, Katya threw out her right arm theatrically, bringing it down in front of her as she bowed, nose touching toes, in graceful gratitude.

Ten minutes later Peter returned, chuckling, and explained that the friend's "house" turned out to be the château opposite the station and that the occupants did not seem to be overly pleased with our agile friend.

For days after, our little village was buzzing with speculation. What was a Russian girl, who did not speak any language except her own, doing at the château? The property had recently been sold and no one had yet been able to establish who the new owners were. The consensus of the men was that Buno now possessed a house of ill, albeit wealthy, repute. It had to be; that was what one read in the newspapers, wasn't it? Russian women were selling themselves everywhere, so why not in Buno?

A few days later a hand-delivered letter arrived in our mailbox. When I opened it I found a thank-you note and two tickets to a dinner and show at the Crazy Horse nightclub in Paris.

Chicken Livers and Green Onions

Serves 4 to 6

- 16 ounces (500 grams) chicken livers
- 8 green onions, chopped
- 2 garlic cloves, finely chopped
- 1/2 tablespoon fresh ginger root, finely chopped
- 1 tablespoon vegetable oil
- 2 tablespoons Chinese rice wine or extra dry vermouth
- 1/2 teaspoon five-spice powder
- 1/2 cup chicken stock
- 1 tablespoon cornstarch
- A little water
- Soy sauce to taste

Fry the garlic and ginger in the oil until soft. Add the rice wine and five-spice powder and fry one minute. Pour in the stock and let simmer for 5 minutes.

Make a paste with the cornstarch and the water and mix into the sauce. Simmer until the sauce thickens.

Add the green onions and chicken livers. Put on a tight lid and let simmer approximately 10 minutes. The livers should be soft and pink inside.

Add soy sauce to taste and serve immediately.

Noodles and Bean Curd

Serves 4 to 6

- *1 pound (500 grams) fresh noodles*
- *1 tablespoon vegetable oil*
- *1 clove garlic, crushed*
- *1/2 tablespoon gingerroot, minced*
- *1 medium leek sliced in rings*
- *1 cup mushrooms, sliced*
- *1 block of bean curd, cut in small cubes*
- *1 tablespoon hoisin sauce*
- *1 tablespoon soy sauce*
- *1 cup bean sprouts*
- *Few sprigs of fresh coriander leaves*

Boil the noodles in water until done, rinse under cold water, and set aside.

In a wok, heat the oil and fry the garlic and the ginger until soft. Add the leek and mushroom slices and stir-fry for 5 minutes. Stir in the bean curd and fry another 5 minutes. Add the hoisin sauce, soy sauce, and noodles and heat through. Add the bean sprouts and fry 1 more minute. Garnish with coriander and serve.

Kiwis and Oranges in Green Ginger Wine

Serves 4 to 6

- *6 oranges*
- *6 kiwis*
- *Dash of five-spice powder*
- *1 measure of green ginger wine (if not available, use 1 measure of whiskey mixed with 1 tablespoon of ginger syrup, or 1 teaspoon of powdered ginger and 1 teaspoon of sugar*

Peel the fruits and cut them into thin slices. Arrange the slices in a fan shape in a round dish, alternating one slice of orange and one of kiwi. Dust the slices with the five-spice powder, and pour the green ginger wine over them. Cover and marinate in a refrigerator for 1 to 2 hours. Serve the fruit topped with the juice of the marinade.

The Gamekeeper

A shot rang out. I flinched, closed my eyes, and screamed. My hand clenched the shoulder where a bullet had entered. Blood was seeping from between my fingers. My own blood, warm and wet, seeping out from where a hot and hungry pain slipped in.

My own voice, screaming, "You are too close," over and over again, until gradually Peter's voice brought me back.

"... two hundred meter limit! ... shot in her shoulder ... hunting accident at eighteen... hysterical ... gun fired this close."

The day had started pleasantly. I was working in the vegetable garden on a mild October morning filled with our village's Sunday sounds. Sparkling laughter of children playing in a treehouse; church bells tolling for a bygone mass; a lawnmower catching on a stone edge. Distant gunshots from the Sunday hunt echoing in the forest.

The morning sun set fire to the amber maples on the hill side, and I stopped digging to admire the changing colors. Colors of Indian spices. The earth smelled of spices. In my mind I revisited the Indian market in Singapore: Serangoon Road, saris, singsong voices calling, "Very fresh, Madum, very good price. Come, I give you special price, Madum."

Then the shot roared in my ears. Serangoon Road dissolved into a beach road on the Dutch coast where a bullet from a straying hunter's gun had buried itself into my shoulder. I relived the terror of that moment in the instant the gun went off.

The sound of Peter's voice slowly brought me back to our garden and to a sheepish looking hunter holding a pheasant that he had shot in the thicket beside our fence. Anger took over from hysteria. I yelled at him that if he did not leave immediately, I would turn his gun on him and on all the other boys with their toys who turn our woods into a combat zone every winter Sunday.

My outcry soon reached the ears of Monsieur le Maire, and the next evening the village gamekeeper and his wife knocked on our door to offer us the hapless bird in atonement. After the introductions and many excuses on behalf of the hunter, we signed the peace treaty with a whisky. Although I liked the stocky, open-faced Laurent and his shy wife, Isabelle, I could not resist voicing my objections to the hunt.

"Do you eat meat?" he wanted to know.

"Well . . . yes."

"I rest my case!" He folded his arms over his chest and flashed a smug smile.

"Wait a minute, you can't compare—"

"Yes, I can. And I can do more. At least this pheasant here had a chance to get away and it enjoyed a life of freedom, an option that is not available for animals raised to end up wrapped in cling film on the shelves of a supermarket."

I found it difficult not to agree with his logic. Still, I do not approve of killing as a sport, and I told him so.

"It is not the killing that is the sport," Laurent argued. "It is being outdoors with your dog, enjoying the wind blowing out the cobwebs. It is watching the clouds racing along a stormy sky. Sometimes I come home without having fired a single shot, but I have had a great day. If a man hunts only to kill, he is not a sportsman."

I opened my mouth for a counterargument but caught a cautioning glance from my partner. Laurent was checked similarly by his wife's pleading eyes, and he abruptly switched the subject to pheasants.

"Pheasants are not native to France. Did you know that?" He glanced at Isabelle to see if he was on the right track and then continued:

"They were introduced from Asia in the early Middle Ages. The male bird was valued for the beauty of its brilliant blue and green feathers, but of course it is the plain-looking young hen that has the finer flesh"—he chuckled, then continued—"and is, of course, best when roasted with wine and spirits. My Isabelle knows how to roast a pheasant, *délicieux*. Tell them how you do it, *ma cherie*. Tell our friends how your grandmother taught you."

"Well, it really isn't all that special." The young, large-boned woman blushed and twirled her thick blond braid. She continued, at first hesitantly, then more confidently in traditional French manner, applying *you* and *your* liberally.

"First you take your *cocotte*. In your *cocotte* you brown your pheasant in some butter, then you flambé it with a small glass of your best cognac. After that, you wrap your bird in slices of bacon, so it does not dry out. Then you put your pan into a very hot oven and add some chicken stock."

"Don't forget the wine, *ma cherie*."

"Oh, yes. A small glass of red wine, and a bay leaf, and—"

"No, no, no, you can't give away your secret ingredient."

Isabelle's large pale blue eyes grew dark with confusion. She resumed twisting her braid.

"But, you said . . . Anyway, it is just a few caraway seeds. What's so special—"

"Poff!" Laurent erupted, slapping his knee, but Isabelle continued serenely.

"When your pheasant is almost done, you add fresh cream to your *cocotte* and baste the bird with this sauce frequently. Then *pffff*"—she bunched her fingertips together and twisted them in a downward motion—"you squeeze a bit of lemon juice, and voilà, you have *faisan à la manière de ma grandmère.* " She opened both hands palms up and smiled triumphantly.

Peter applauded her finale and then suggested that maybe we should put grandmother's theory into present practice.

"All this talk about food has made me hungry." He looked at Laurent and ordained: "You'll stay for dinner, of course, so that Isabelle can supervise the preparation à la grandmère."

"What? But that's impossible." Laurent stared at Peter in disbelief. "You can't cook a freshly killed pheasant. It has to hang for at least three days." He narrowed his eyes and looked at us sternly.

"You don't know anything about game, do you?"

Peter shook his head.

"I thought so. You probably do not know how to clean a pheasant either? No, no don't apologize."

He walked into the kitchen and put the bird back into the plastic bag in which he had carried it.

"I'll take care of your pheasant at home and return it toward the end of the week."

He came back into the living room and sat down. Turning to me he said:

"Tonight we will have to eat something else."

Isabelle quickly offered to help in the kitchen to smooth over her husband's clumsy manners.

One hour later she carried our dinner to the table and announced ceremoniously: "May I present *Coquelet à l'Origan à la*

Manière d'Yvonne accompanied by *Gratin de Courgettes et Pommes de Terre.*"

Isabelle served Laurent a small portion of each. After his first careful bites, he reached over and said while serving himself a larger helping, "*C'est pas mal, ça!*" This is not bad.

Three days later Laurent returned with the trussed pheasant and a small ragged-edged, leather-bound book, its title long since erased.

"Your roasted chicken was delicious, and since you said you were interested in traditional French food, Isabelle thought you might enjoy reading her grandmother's *Cuisinière Bourgeoise*. Keep it as long as you like."

When he had left, I carefully opened the little book. Inside the cover someone had written in elegant, curly letters:

"To Ange Debond, on her birthday, August 15, 1784." Isabelle had trusted me with a family heirloom.

That evening I prepared *faifan au foleil*, a recipe that Ange, or maybe a great-granddaughter, had marked as *"delifieux."* The pheasant was indeed delicious, but we had befriended the enemy and the *faifan* took its revenge: It caused such a vicious food poisoning, that we vowed never to eat pheasant again.

Pheasants are nesting in our garden now, on the safe side of the fence.

Roasted Oregano Chicken

Serves 4

- *2 spring chickens or Cornish game hens*

For the marinade:
- *1 bunch fresh oregano*
- *1 tablespoon coarse-grain mustard*
- *1 tablespoon balsamic vinegar*
- *1 clove garlic*
- *1 teaspoon salt*
- *1/3 cup good quality oil*

Mix all the ingredients for the marinade in a blender until smooth. Halve the chickens and coat with the marinade. Marinate for at least three hours. Then roast them on a rack in the oven at 170 degrees C. (350 degrees F.) for 45 minutes, or until done.

Zucchini and Potato Layer

Serves 4

- *3 medium zucchini, sliced*
- *4 medium potatoes, thinly sliced*
- *1 clove garlic, pressed*
- *2 tablespoons chopped fresh oregano or thyme*
- *1/3 cup crème fraîche*
- *Slices of mature Gouda or cheddar*
- *Salt and pepper to taste.*

In an ovenproof dish, arrange the slices of zucchini and potato alternately in a fan pattern. Season with pepper and salt. Spread the garlic over the slices and top with the chopped fresh herbs. Over this spread the crème fraîche. Bake in the oven at 170 degrees C. (350 degrees F.) for 30 minutes, or until the potatoes are done. Cover with the slices of cheese, and grill until the cheese starts to brown.

Ruby Tuesday

When I think of Ruby Tuesday I am always reminded of one particular Christmas Eve and a dinner that Daniel doesn't care to remember.

Each year, in the two weeks before Christmas, Daniel drives up from Gascony, hauling a tattered trailer stocked with jars of politically incorrect foie gras and similar festive delicacies that he sells to his established clientele in the Paris area. Apart from the fragrant melons that he brings in August, these home-produced cholesterol boosters represent most of his yearly earnings. On both visits he parks his trailer in our locked courtyard in exchange for some of his products.

Daniel is an aging French hippie. Long after his contemporaries had returned from the countryside to become money manipulators and spending seducers, he was still holding out on his Ardèche farm without running water or electricity. Finally, after catching pneumonia a second time, he left the harsh Ardèche winters in favor of the milder weather in Gascony and began the slow restoration of a farm that had been abandoned some hundred years before. He remains a free spirit, bound neither by society nor by daily bathing, which might be why Ruby Tuesday is quite fond of him.

Ruby Tuesday is a frequent houseguest at Lastenfurst and shares Daniel's contempt for the tub. But then, Ruby Tuesday is a border collie. Like most dogs, she enjoys barking at passersby and has an endless desire to retrieve sticks and Frisbees, but this is where her normality ends.

Ruby is an erudite dog, enraptured by jazz and classical music. When she does not care for a certain arrangement, she noses the buttons on the CD player in protest. In her canine mind, the sound system is also the direct source of lights and shadows. She will drop everything, even a tummy scratch, to leap at a moving shadow or a shimmering reflection. This particular behavior has led to the suspicion by her humans that she embodies the spirit of Claude Monet.

Like Monet, Ruby is a tyrant, demanding a *son et lumière*, especially at dinnertime. Opening the dining room cupboard or picking up a box of matches to light the dinner candles provokes a mad dervish whirl and an impatient bark for the show to begin. Visiting friends obligingly reflect the light from their watches or create shadows on the wall, to the amusement of both dog and humans.

Monet's fastidious supervision of his gardeners at Giverny was legendary, and in the same way Ruby watches intently and critically as we labor at the mammoth task of turning our acre of dying forest into a "place that the eye of heaven visits." The eye of Ruby however, is most vigilant in the vegetable plot, for like Monet, Ruby Tuesday is a gourmand.

A few years ago at Christmastime, Ruby Tuesday was introduced to Daniel. She instantly included him in her daily supervision routine. Every morning he would let himself into our courtyard to take out the orders for that day from his trailer. Ruby would play shadow, following every move as Daniel neatly stacked the boxes and then loaded them into his car. Every now and again he'd step back and stumble over her, muttering that the blasted animal was an effective alternative to superglue.

This ritual took place every morning just until Christmas Eve, when Daniel came over to share the traditional French Christmas meal with us.

Dirty Dan had washed for the occasion and came early to help prepare the dinner. While he fussed over the oysters and the foie gras, he entertained me with a running commentary on the principles of preparing a fresh duck liver and the aesthetic details of presentation.

"You must be sure to choose a liver that is supple and has a clear color. Not a single trace of blood, however minute, must be seen. You understand?"

He looked at me sternly over his glasses to see if I was paying attention.

"Then you take your liver like this." He cupped his hands like a child carefully holding a newborn kitten.

"You place it on your cutting board. Separate the two lobes with your sharpest knife and remove all the sinews. Salt it slightly with freshly ground sea salt, add a small glass of Sauternes, and cook it in your oven, medium heat, for about fifteen minutes. Never overcook a foie gras. Remove the liver from the oven and leave it to cool for half an hour.

"Then, my very good friend, it is time for my secret seasoning. Mix some freshly ground salt and pepper and add two tablespoons of grilled sourdough breadcrumbs. Sprinkle this mixture over the liver, put it in a terrine, one lobe covering the other. Weigh it down with something heavy and leave it in the refrigerator for one day. The next day, you dip the terrine in hot water, turn it over, and unmold it over your cutting board. Now we are ready to slice it."

A small piece crumbled off as he sliced the foie.

"Here, try this, and after you have descended from heaven, tell me what you think."

"The best I've ever eaten, but you lied to me."

Daniel shot me a half-amused, half-hurt look.

"You did not use Sauternes but Jurançon, and you used Chinese five-spice powder instead of pepper."

"Maybe I did, maybe I did not." He grinned. "What on earth are you putting in that sauce?"

He sniffed at my jar of mahonia jelly and curled up his nose in suspicion.

"Mahonia jelly," I replied casually, concentrating on my sauce, inspired by Daniel's choice of spice.

"Mahonia jelly? Of course. Mahonia jelly."

He grabbed the jar and carried it into the living room. Waving the jar in the air, he announced loudly to our friends who had arrived a few minutes earlier, "Our hostess uses mahonia jelly. It's so obvious, dear guests. Who would not use mahonia jelly on Christmas Eve?"

As he brought back my jar, he pleaded, "What, for the love of our gourmet God, is mahonia jelly?"

"Jelly made from the berries of *Mahonia aquifolium*, the shrub you see growing outside the kitchen door. It has lovely clusters of fragrant yellow flowers in winter and edible berries during early summer. I have to share them with the blackbirds, who consider them their favorite food. Try some."

Daniel sampled the jelly, moving a spoonful of it around his palate, inhaling through his nose as if testing a vintage wine.

"Your blackbird berries . . . a sprig of rosemary . . . Marc de Bourgogne . . . some chili. Unusual, but not bad."

He scattered sprigs of chives over the plate with foie gras, then took another sample of the Mahonia jelly, mumbling to himself, "Not bad, actually, Daniel, not bad at all. Could be great with game and duck. Perhaps also with foie gras?"

He scooped out small amounts of the jelly and creatively placed them around the slices of foie gras. When he finished the decoration of his masterpiece, he proudly showed the plate to the guests, who were playfully casting rabbit and spider shadows on the wall for Ruby Tuesday. She and our friends stopped their game to admire Daniel's artistry. Accompanied by exclamations of admiration and anticipation, he carried the plate back into the kitchen, where he decreed:

"First we shall have the oysters and a glass of Champagne. Only then, my impatient friends, only then shall we have the foie gras."

Conversation, fired by the Champagne, erupted and flowed easily, meandering through favorite restaurants, the latest novel by Duras, wines, France's angst over the eroding purity of her language, and the monumental maintenance costs of the Pompidou Centre. The evening was off to a good start, and after the conversation had returned to restaurants, Daniel opened some bottles of Jurançon and announced that the time had arrived to sample his pièce de résistance.

As he got up, he stumbled over Ruby, who had superglued herself onto him for the last ten minutes, staring at him with adoring eyes in complete submission.

He disappeared into the kitchen, gently scolding Ruby, when all of a sudden we heard him explode.

"*No!* Oh, no. Disaster. This is not possible. Ruby, you didn't. Oh, no. This, this dog—this *thief.*"

I found a dejected Daniel in the kitchen, holding his plate, its decoration neatly in place around a clean and shining empty space where the foie gras had been. Ruby was sitting in front of him, imploring clemency, but our friend was too distraught to be angry. The reason for Daniel's distress was not that simple.

In the week before Christmas, Daniel and I had a discussion on why we enjoy cooking for others. He had explained that the only way he knew how to dress some of the wounds caused by social and political injustice was through his cooking.

"So people forget to be angry for a little while. So they will laugh and talk to each other. Maybe they even listen to each other, and with a bit of luck they go home and share the goodwill around. I put a lot of effort in these." He nodded at the jars waiting to be loaded into the car. "Quality kindles attention, and when you pay attention you become still. To experience peace, you need to be still. This is what I put into these jars at Christmastime."

When I saw a very peaceful border collie attentively looking up at Daniel, I conceded that his Christmas message had been received loud and clear. If not just by Ruby Tuesday.

Christmas Duck
Serves 4 to 6

- 19 ounces (600 grams) duck breast, thinly sliced and cut into 25-milli-meter strips
- 1/2 teaspoon five-spice powder
- 1 tablespoon butter
- 1/2 cup bunching onions
- 1 tablespoon minced fresh sage
- 2 tablespoons mahonia or cranberry jelly
- 1/2 cup crème fraîche
- 1 teaspoon soy sauce
- 1/2 teaspoon five-spice powder
- Few drops of Tabasco (optional)
- Sage leaves for garnish

Season the duck with the five-spice powder. Sauté the duck strips in the butter for 3 minutes. Reserve and keep warm. Slice the onions. In the butter, fry the onion with the sage until the onions are transparent. Add the mahonia jelly, and stir to incorporate. Stir in the crème fraîche, soy, five-spice powder, and Tabasco. Add the duck to the sauce and warm through. Serve garnished with a few sage leaves.

Carrot Purée With Chervil

Serves 4 to 6

- *14 ounces (400 grams) carrots, washed and scraped*
- *2 garlic cloves, peeled*
- *Slice of fresh gingerroot*
- *2 tablespoons crème fraîche*
- *2 tablespoons fresh chervil, chopped*
- *1/2 tablespoon sweet butter*
- *Freshly ground sea salt and pepper to taste*
- *Sprig of chervil for garnish*

Boil the carrots, garlic, and ginger in a little water until the carrots are tender but not soft. Drain off the water and discard the slice of ginger. In a blender, purée the carrots, garlic, crème fraîche, and chervil until smooth. Return to the pan, add the butter, stir, and warm through. Add salt and pepper to taste. Serve, decorated with a sprig of chervil.

Pears Baked in Benedictine

Serves 4

- *4 dessert pears, peeled, but leave the stems*
- *4 half-teaspoons honey*
- *4 half-tablespoons Benedictine or Grand Marnier*
- *4 generous dollops of vanilla ice cream*
- *For choc-a-holics: 4 tablespoons hot chocolate sauce*
- *4 sheets extra strong aluminum foil*

Put each pear on a sheet of foil and drizzle with the honey and liqueur. Close the parcels and bake for 30 to 45 minutes at 180 degrees C. (360 degrees F.). Open the parcels stem side up, top each pear with the ice cream, and drizzle with the chocolate sauce.

Monsieur Herblot

Every day at three o'clock, Monsieur Herblot shuffles past our front gate on his daily walk through our village. He pokes his head into our garden, and if he finds someone there, he'll take off his cap and say, "Good day to you, Monsieur, Madame. You are working in your garden? One has to take advantage of the weather, because it is not what it used to be, I can assure you. We used to have . . ."

If it rains, the weather never used to be as wet. When it is dry, he'll predict the worst drought in the history of Buno. Distrustful of authority, he wags a gnarled finger at the sky and adds, "The government is messing about with our climate, Monsieur. There used to be plenty of rain at this time of year."

Most days he ends his lamentation with the words "The farmers are facing difficult times, Madame, very difficult. It is a miracle that our cows are still producing milk."

Monsieur Herblot is ninety-five years old and has bumbled beyond our restrictions of time. His mind is wandering in and out of an era long before the Beauce farmers had the financial means to go on strike. Agribusiness has long since replaced mixed farming, but the old man still worries about late frosts that destroy apple blossoms and viruses that attack the "Gâtinaise" chickens. When he totters through the lanes, he does not see that the last neglected apple orchard flaunts a notice: "For sale. Plot with permission to build."

Then suddenly, he will reenter our time and lament the loss of "all good Gâtinais products."

"We used to produce France's sweetest honey, and there was no finer rabbit than the one grown right here in the Gâtinais."

One day Monsieur Herblot arrived at our gate with three trout wrapped in a newspaper. Jabbing his finger through the paper he croaked, "My girl who works at the wood factory told me to bring these."

His "girl" at the wood factory is now seventy-two and lives on the coast. The wood factory closed down a decade ago.

Old Herblot never fished in his life. Just who it was who had given him the trout, he could not say. Leaning on his walking stick, he mumbled a few words to himself and shook his head.

"The wife never prepared fish, but I have always loved trout."

As he had brought three fish, I invited him to stay for lunch, and after a glass of red wine ("pinard" to the locals) he came back to the nineties and warmed to a conversation about the local farming history.

"Each farm had at least three hundred chickens, and most of them only raised the Gâtinaise. The best Parisian restaurants cooked with the Gâtinaise. Tell me, have you ever seen a Gâtinaise in Milly market? No, Madame, they have all but disappeared. And do they still fatten chickens with oats cooked in milk?

"Corn," he scoffed. "Yellow meat, that's what you get when you feed them corn. A chicken must have white meat."

During our conversation he had hobbled behind me into the vegetable garden and watched me pick yellow French beans, chrysanthemum leaves, and the herbs that would accompany the trout. He approved of the beans, crushed the chrysanthemum leaves between his fingers and smelled.

"Mustard!" he judged. "Used to grow a different kind around here. Used to grow a different mint around here too. Now they ship out one hundred twenty tonnes of this Mitcham mint a year. I hope they are sending it right back to America. The *Ancienne Milly* is far superior to this foreign weed."

Our guest voiced his disapproval of foreign imports once again. He does so almost every time we speak, so I smiled sweetly and teased, "Then Monsieur does not approve of us living here?"

"But you are from Buno, are you not?"

He cackled and coughed and cackled again. "Yes, yes, from Buno . . . Just like old Herblot . . . From Buno."

Once back in the kitchen he asked for another glass of pinard and resumed chuckling while I prepared our lunch.

During our meal Monsieur Herblot drifted in and out of the present. Sometimes he described in detail which new fertilizers were being tested at the research farm on the plateau. A moment later he worried about the vineyard on the hill. This last vineyard had been ripped up more than sixty years ago.

"I do like my pinard, although she would not let me drink it."
"She?"
"The wife, she would not let me smoke either . . . and then all these people at the funeral."
"Funeral?"
"The wife's funeral. Old Castanier came up to me, telling me how sorry he was and all that. 'This must be the saddest day in your life, Herblot,' he told me.

" 'Saddest day in my life?' I said. 'Saddest day in my life? Dear Castanier, this is the happiest day in my life.'" His back straightened.

"For thirty years that woman made my life hell. Every day she yelled at me. 'Don't smoke, Herblot. Don't drink, Herblot. Discipline your children, Herblot. You don't earn enough, Herblot. I am ill because of you, Herblot.'"

His eyes lit up with anger, his bent fingers formed into fists.

"She was never ill, Madame. Never. I had to wait until I was eighty before I finally gained my freedom, Madame. But I vowed to live out those thirty years she stole from me. I will drink my pinard and smoke my pipe until I am a hundred and ten."

When I see old Monsieur Herblot shuffling past our house each day he seems determined to fulfill his pledge. Sometimes he misses out a day and I worry, but he always returns. He pokes his head around the gate, crinkles a crooked eye, and says, "Good day to you, Madame. You are working in your garden? One has to take advantage of the weather . . ."

Trout Marinated in Rosemary

Serves 4

- *4 pink trout*

For the marinade:
- *1/4 cup tightly packed fresh rosemary leaves*
- *1 teaspoon freshly ground sea salt*
- *2 garlic cloves*
- *Juice of half a lemon*
- *1/4 cup grapeseed oil*
- *1/2 tablespoon Dijon mustard*

Blend all the ingredients for the marinade until smooth, and steep the fish in the mixture for 4 hours. Barbecue the fish over charcoal on both sides until done. Baste with marinade while cooking.

French Beans With Chrysanthemum Leaves

Serves 4

- *18 ounces (500 grams) young French beans, parboiled*
- *1 tablespoon butter*
- *1 cup mushrooms, wiped clean and thinly sliced*
- *6 spring onions*
- *2 tablespoons fresh dill, chopped*
- *3 tablespoons crème fraîche*
- *1 cup young oriental chrysanthemum leaves (or mustard greens or chard)*
- *Freshly ground black pepper and sea salt*

Fry the mushrooms and the white parts of the onions in the butter until soft and all liquid is released. Add the beans, dill, and crème fraîche and season to taste.

Mix the warm vegetables with the chrysanthemum leaves and serve immediately.

The Necromancer

Each year in early spring we make a special trip deep into the Fontainebleau Forest to gather young bracken tips. American friends call them fiddleheads because of their appearance, but I prefer to call them spring-sprongs. They taste of crisp spring days, of asparagus, and of wild mushrooms.

If the weather is mild, we plan a picnic on one of the highest points in the forest. From the top of this prehistoric tropical sand dune the view stretches over wooded valleys, sandy plains, and capricious clusters of rocks and caves. We think of it as our secret place, as it is hidden away in the less-visited area of the Trois Pignons.

One fine spring morning we went spring-spronging with friends from London. I had packed a light lunch and two bottles of Mercurey to celebrate the first mild Sunday of the year.

We set off on narrow paths through bracken and heather. Gradually the trail disappeared, and we scrambled the last hundred meters through junipers and brambles.

"You know, I've never seen another living soul in all the times I've been here," Peter said. "We're only seventy kilometers from Paris. There is no place this close to London, where you can be alone and away from it all." He untangled himself from the last bit of bramble bush and climbed up to our rock. Arms outstretched and scanning the wide view, he continued, "Et voilà, mes amis, la forêt de Fontainebleau! Not a single trace of another human being."

"Do wild boar go camping?" inquired Daphne, who was investigating a cave just below our viewpoint. "Come and have a look at this."

We clambered down to join her. She pointed at a mangy blanket, various plastic bags, and a small smouldering campfire. "Who would—"

Just then an imperious voice behind us commanded, "Remove yourselves immediately from my abode. This is my forest. Now go!"

We turned to find ourselves face to face with a scrawny, unkempt man whose appearance belied his elocution. Thin strands of unwashed hair streaked across his face as he flapped his arms about him. "You are trespassing. I must insist, be away, or I shall have to do battle!"

Paul, who teaches literature in London, rummaged around in our picnic basket, pulled out one of the burgundies, and asked,

"Would Don Quixote care for a glass of wine as proof of our peaceful intentions?"

Our knight stopped flailing and answered in fluent, albeit accented English, "Don Quixote you may think I am. Nay, 'tis a mere necromancer who gladly accepts your offer of amity."

Paul poured out a glass. The necromancer put the wine to his lips, took a small sip, whirled it around in his mouth, and swallowed.

"I dare say, 'tis a rare treat in Henri's Fôret de Bière."

Daphne concluded that Don Quixote's name was Henri. She wanted to know more.

"Henry, why do you call this the Beer Forest?"

"My lovely lady, *Bière* does not refer to the golden liquid but rather to bruyère, which is the heather that has rendered these hills the color purple in late autumn even before Henri and I aimed our arrows at wild boars and noble deer."

He bowed graciously toward Daphne, blinking at a strand of hair that had wriggled its way into his left eye.

"Henry?"

"Mistaken identity again, I'm afraid. I speak of Henri the First." He swiped at the defiant lock of hair with the back of his hand, sipped his wine, and sighed.

"Almost a thousand years ago now. Crusades . . . tournaments . . . my king loved the hunt most of all. We would tether the horses at Bliaud's spring—"

"Bliaud's spring?" Peter interrupted. "La fontaine de Bliaud?" He turned to the necromancer. "Bliaud's spring is Fontainebleau?"

"That's the name Louis recorded in his charts. Louis the Seventh, you understand. Anyway, just as well, because Bliaud was a bandit."

Paul moved his glasses up and down the bridge of his nose with his right hand. He often does this when he is about to ask a caustic question. The necromancer turned to him and smiled.

"You marvel at my detailed knowledge of the past, learned sir? May I suggest to you that limitations of time are but an illusion?

A necromancer is a realist."

Paul left his glasses at the tip of his nose.

"I'll give you proof."

He glanced at our picnic basket and continued.

"I've had a vision. I saw myself seated on a rock partaking in a halcyon repast with two gentle ladies and their handsome cavaliers." He took another sip of wine and flashed a persuasive smile at me over the rim of his glass. I burst out laughing, invited him to our picnic, and began to unpack the basket. Paul's glasses resumed sliding up and down his nose as he recited to our 'guest':

"What neat repast shall feast you—"

Cutting him short, the necromancer continued: "Light and choice, of Attic taste?"

The glasses slid to an abrupt halt.

He accepted a piece of rabbit, took a small bite, savored it, and beamed at Paul.

"An appropriate quote, friend in letters. The seasoning of this rabbit would have pleased John." He paused to take another bite and said whilst chewing, "Thyme for life's energy. Virgil took it in his salads. It invigorated him. Even flavored his cheese with it. He liked to chew mustard seeds with his meat."

The necromancer continued to accurately name all the ingredients I had used in the marinade for the rabbit. He mentioned that Virgil also wrote about bruising garlic and wild thyme "for 'the mowers wearied with the fierce heat.' Oh, and Pliny suggested garlic as an aphrodisiac."

He spoke with authority and intimacy, as if he had known the Roman writers in person.

After our lunch he fell into a conversation about the forest. Peter reasoned that Fontainebleau Forest was managed properly, with no large areas of clear felling and a good range of tree species of different ages. At this point the necromancer looked at Paul and said with slight sarcasm in his voice, "This is the forest primeval."

Paul took off his glasses, smiled broadly, and replied, "Longfellow. *Evangeline*."

"Quite so," agreed our lunch guest. He turned to Peter, who carried on where he had left off.

"When I studied in Edinburgh, we were always told that the French are the world leaders in forestry."

"I am in direct contact with world leaders," the literary man interrupted. "Only this morning I told Clinton in a telepathic message that he should leave the White House immediately." He scrunched up his eyes and continued in a conspiratorial tone. "I informed him that there will be an attempt on his life. Do not alarm yourselves. Bill took my advice. He and his family have left."

We fell silent as the necromancer jabbered on about his council to Nixon to end the Vietnam war. He had warned the Argentine government about Maggie's strong will. He advised Bush during the invasion of Kuwait, and he tried convincing Saddam to stop persecuting the Kurds.

"And my task is not yet finished." He motioned us to come closer, put his index finger to his lips, and whispered, "I'll disclose the true reason for my sojourn under the greenwood tree. You are aware that three lives have been cut short here last month?"

We had indeed read that a Scandinavian couple had been found murdered in the woods behind a nearby restaurant. Their dog had been shot also. The police suspected a drug-related vendetta and had not been able to find the murderers. The necromancer went on to explain that "they" had called him to find the killers.

"They?"

"The spirits of the murdered ones." He looked about him and said, "If anyone should ask you about me, just say you met a fool in the forest, a motley fool."

Paul grinned over his glasses at the little man. "As you like it."

The seer smiled. "And now I must attend to my task. I thank you, sweet lady, for my sustenance." He kissed my hand, picked up a tattered book from the cave, and walked away into his forest.

Paul called after him. "Fare thee well! And if forever, still forever fare thee well."

He turned around slowly, lifted his shoulders and shouted,

"Byron!" He waved and walked on.

That evening we heard on the BBC radio that an armed man had tried to get into the White House. The CIA had been forewarned and had moved Clinton and his family away before the attack took place.

Rabbit in Mustard Marinade

Serves 4

- 1 rabbit, cut into 8 pieces
- 2 tablespoons unsalted butter

For the marinade:
- 1 tablespoon fresh thyme leaves
- 1 tablespoon good quality mustard
- 1 teaspoon honey
- 1/2 teaspoon ground coriander
- 2 teaspoons sea salt
- Freshly ground pepper
- 1 garlic clove
- 1/2 cup cream
- Sprigs of thyme for garnish

Blend all the ingredients for the marinade in a mixer until smooth. Marinate the rabbit pieces 4 hours or overnight in the refrigerator. Remove the rabbit from the marinade, wipe and dry with a paper towel. Reserve the marinade.

Fry the rabbit in the hot butter, 2 minutes on each side. Lower the heat and put the marinade in the pan with the rabbit. Simmer for about 30 minutes or until the rabbit is tender and the marinade is dry. Serve hot or cold, served with a few sprigs of thyme.

Tagliatelli Salad
Serves 4

- 1 red onion, chopped
- 1/2 cup mushrooms, sliced
- 2 tablespoons grapeseed oil
- 1/2 cup blanched French beans
- 4 tablespoons crème fraîche

Dressing:
- 1 garlic clove, crushed
- 1/2 teaspoon salt
- 1/2 tablespoon Dijon mustard
- 2 tablespoons sherry vinegar
- 4 tablespoons walnut oil
- 4 tablespoons grapeseed oil
- 1/2 cup fresh basil

- 16 ounces (400 grams) fresh tagliatelli
- 1/2 cup blanched snow peas
- 1/2 cup chopped red and yellow pepper
- Small bunch fresh basil leaves
- 1/4 cup toasted pine nuts
- Freshly ground black pepper
- A few borage flowers and pine nuts for garnish

Fry the onion and the mushrooms in the oil until soft. Add the beans and crème fraîche and cook 2 minutes on low heat. Allow to cool.

Mix all ingredients for the dressing in a blender until smooth.

Cook the pasta for 3 minutes in salted, boiling water, drain, and mix with the dressing. Toss all ingredients, and garnish with a few borage flowers and pine nuts.

Ray's Walnut Tart

Tart shell:
- 1/2 cup unsalted butter
- 1/4 cup brown sugar
- 1 egg yolk
- 1 cup all-purpose flour

Filling:
- 2 cups coarsely chopped walnuts
- 1/2 cup brown sugar, packed
- 1/4 cup dark corn syrup
- 1/4 cup heavy cream
- 2 egg yolks
- 1/4 cup unsalted butter

For the shell:
Beat the butter and sugar until light and fluffy. Add the egg yolk and beat well. Gradually beat in the flour until well mixed (it should be crumbly). Preheat the oven to 375 degrees F. (190 degrees C.). Form the dough into a ball and press evenly into a 9-inch (22-centimeter) tart pan with removable bottom. Bake for 12 minutes, until lightly browned. Cool on a wire rack.

For the filling:
Sprinkle the walnuts in the tart shell. Beat the sugar, syrup, cream, and egg yolks until creamy. Heat the butter in a small saucepan and stir into the sugar mixture. Pour over the walnuts. Bake at 375 degrees F. (190 degrees C.) in the center of oven for 10 minutes or until the mixture is bubbly. Serve at room temperature.

Michel Bras

Diverse in opinion as the French are, they agree on one thing: "To eat well is to live well." People will drive a long distance to a restaurant with a good reputation, and the discovery of an excellent *petite auberge* is always shared among friends.

"Ah, you are going to Lyon? I know this little restaurant not far from . . ."

"*Alors*, you are going to Montpellier on your holiday?"

Alex walked into our kitchen, a map of the Massif Central stuffed hastily into his jacket. He had just returned from Clermont-Ferrand and was eager to share his discovery of a small restaurant near Issoire with us. He spread the map on the table and traced the A75 with his finger.

"Clermont-Ferrand . . . go south . . . you see Issoire? Leave the A75 . . . go south . . . onto the D996. Somewhere around here is a small village . . . Sarpoil, here it is."

Triumphantly he jabbed his finger several times at the map.

"Sarpoil, that's it. I ate at this auberge." He kissed the tips of four fingers on his right hand, then yanked them away from his mouth and observed them intently. "The chef used to cook for the Ritz in Paris. You must go there."

We accepted Alex's gracious gift, and that night we replanned our route toward Montpellier with another three of four "stomach stopovers" in mind. Two out-of-date Gault Millau and Michelin guides served as appetizers.

"Where shall we stop after Alex's restaurant?"

I bent over the map, refound the A75 and Issoire. "Let's see, south, the Aubrac, empty hills, primitive and wild country. How does that sound to you?"

"Any good places to eat?"

On the map I found a red stripe under Laguiole.

"Laguiole," read the Michelin guide," home of the Laguiole knife. Altitude: 1004 meters. Important cattle and cheese markets. Winter sport centre. Fabulous views towards the Cantal and the Aubrac."

I had known about the beautiful knives. When boys come of age in France, they are given a "Laguiole" (pronounced Laïole). However, in the mists of my memory lingered a description of wild herbs, plants, and spices. I picked up the Gault Millau Guide and read:

"Laguiole, home of Michel Bras." Of course! I suddenly remembered reading an article about Michel Bras when he was chosen France's chef of the year. Hidden in one of the remotest parts of the country, he had become famous overnight when Christian Millau discovered him in 1980 and awarded him his highest accolades. For years after, the major chefs in France snubbed him, as Michel had no formal culinary training. Only after the young chef had won the "Best Chef in France" award in 1991 did they reluctantly venture out to the Aubrac in order to say, "I ate chez Michel Bras."

I continued reading Millau's lyrical description.

". . . unparalleled grace and sensuous intellect . . . a kitchen burst forth from the fields like a pure spring. . . botanist chef with the metaphysical dash of a Zen follower . . . true artist who knows that nothing is more difficult than simplicity . . ."

The guide described Michel as a shy perfectionist who only leaves his kitchen to run marathons and to collect wild herbs and plants in the mountains of his beloved Aubrac. The guide also suggested that Michel's breakfasts were "heavenly" and worth staying overnight for, as long as one "does not mind the simple, inexpensive hotel rooms."

We phoned to make our reservations.

"Our rooms are one thousand francs a night, and our menus

range from two hundred to six hundred francs."

Monsieur Millau and I did not agree on the price of "simple, inexpensive hotel rooms." Peter folded his hands to one side of his face, closing his eyes, and shook his head. He then pointed at his stomach and nodded eagerly.

"We would like to make a reservation for dinner."

It was with slight misgivings that we arrived in Laguiole a week later and parked in front of the address given in the guide.

"But Madame, Michel Bras moved to the Route d'Aubrac years ago," said the manager of an elegant gift shop selling Michel Bras kitchenware and delicacies. "I'll phone to say that you are slightly delayed."

"I'm sure it's a snob place now," muttered Peter as we drove along a wild and empty road. "That's the problem. As soon as a chef becomes famous it goes to his head. The food is bound to be disappointing too."

Just then we noticed a building ablaze with bright lights on top of the next hill. Our spirits sank. It was going to be a snob place after all.

Leaving our ten-year-old dented Honda amid lustrous Porsches and Jaguars, we began to climb the winding path toward the restaurant. Our spirits lifted gently as we went up the trail between the wide open views of the Aubrac. We turned a corner, and from beyond the native herbs the building suddenly leaped out of the hillside toward the setting sun. The stage was set.

We dined suspended between basalt rock and honeyed sky. Each course revealed Michel's close affinity to the hills of his birth: trout with young yarrow tips; lamb and ramson; tender tops of garlic mustard; *crème glacée* perfumed with acacia flowers.

After dinner we strolled down the path, inhaling the intense scent of mountain herbs in the cool evening air. Michel Bras had treated us to a feast for all our senses. He had introduced us to his world, his discovery of the fragrance and flavors of nature. He had given us new sensations and new tastes to contemplate.

Under the immense sky of the Aubrac we felt close to the heavens.

I am growing garlic mustard now, and just among friends: If you happen to be near Laguiole, I know this wonderful restaurant . . .

Scrambled Eggs With Herbs
Serves 4

- 6 eggs
- 1 tablespoon crème fraîche
- Pepper
- Salt
- 1 tablespoon butter
- 2 tablespoons young garlic mustard tops, chopped (or chives, although the flavor is not the same)
- 1 tablespoon cream

In a bowl, whisk the eggs and the crème fraîche with a fork. Season with pepper and salt. Melt the butter in a pan and scramble the egg mixture until it is slightly firm. Add the chopped herbs and incorporate. Add the cream to stop the cooking. Serve decorated with a few sprigs of garlic mustard.

Wild Mushroom Açorda

Serves 4

- 18 ounces (500 grams) wild mushrooms, such as field (Agaricus ampester) or parasol mushrooms (Lepiota rocera); or use dried mushrooms soaked in warm water for 20 minutes and heated in a pan until they release all their fluid
- 1 tablespoon butter
- 1 garlic clove, finely chopped
- 3 tablespoons heavy cream
- 10 fluid ounces (300 mililiters) vegetable stock
- 1 Swedish rye cracker, pounded into crumbs
- Salt and pepper to taste

Wipe the mushrooms clean with a moist cloth (never soak in water; doing so will spoil their taste and consistency). Remove the stems and cut the caps into four. If you have only a few wild mushrooms, or are using dried ones, make up the bulk with cultivated mushrooms, as they will take up the flavor of the wild ones. Maximum flavor at minimum expense!

Melt the butter in a pan and fry the mushrooms with the garlic until they have released their liquid. Reserve a few choice pieces to decorate the açorda.

Add the cream, stock, and cracker crumbs and simmer for 5 minutes.

Transfer the mixture to a food processor and blend until smooth.

Return to the pan and warm through. Serve decorated with the reserved mushroom pieces.

August Fifteenth

But my dear lady, today is the fifteenth of August; our hotel is fully booked."

Noticing the look of incomprehension on my face, the receptionist explained: "Assumption ... a national holiday in France."

We had traveled down from Angers thinking we would find a charming hotel in the Sologne to celebrate Peter's birthday. It being a Wednesday, we had not counted on hotels being full.

A young American couple arrived and received the same message.

"If you don't mind a small but romantic hotel, I can take you there. My friend Yvette runs it."

The four of us readily agreed and followed our guide's tiny Citroën down to a lost building surrounded by forest.

Yvette welcomed us with open arms, which she promptly wrapped around me whilst staring at me lovingly.

"I have a wonderful double bed for you. Unfortunately I cannot be with you this evening. I have to assist at a wedding"

She looked sadly into my eyes and swore she would attend to me in the morning.

The young couple turned to me and grinned. "Hm, excuse me, but since she loves you so passionately, could you ask her if she has a wonderful double bed for us as well?"

Yvette answered in accented English before I had a chance to open my mouth. "Yes, you can have the last room. It's next to this charming lady's."

She turned to leave, paused, and added, "You will have to be patient at dinner. Most of my staff are helping out at the wedding. There is only the chef and his young girlfriend, who is new to the job of serving tables."

Indeed, Adèle panicked as she tried to follow her chef's orders and also tend to people's need for a glass of wine. When she finally brought the chef's special dish of *pintade* to our table, she struggled to open a bottle of Burgundy. Peter took pity on her and valiantly opened it. She admitted not knowing anything about wine other than the fact there was red, white, and rosé. Peter knew more, draped a white napkin over his right arm, and took over as the wine waiter for the evening.

He explained to the young American couple that *pintade* was guinea fowl and roasted red beets were just the right accompaniment.

During my solitary spells at our table our new friends started chatting to me.

I learned that Duane had been in France on a project since January and this was the first time his fiancé had been able to come for a visit. He had picked her up from Charles de Gaulle airport that morning and had hoped to find a typical French countryside hotel, enjoy a romantic candlelight dinner, and catch up on eight months of lost time.

This last fact became rather evident after we retired to our adjacent rooms for the night. We coughed politely to alert them that the wall separating our double beds was very thin indeed. A lot of whisperings such as "Oh, no, they can hear us" and "What do we do now?" ensued, but eventually Duane announced, "I am sorry, but you know, oh what the heck."

Hardly had the night gone quiet when there was an urgent tapping on our bedroom window. A muffled voice implored, "Can you please let us in? The hotel is locked."

Peter opened the curtain and looked into two pairs of pleading eyes.

"I am sorry, but I don't know who you are. Besides I do not have a key to the door either."

"Well, we are in room number six. If you don't believe us, just go to the room and you will find our children sleeping there."

From beside us Duane asked, "Hey, what's going on out there?" I explained the situation, and he volunteered to check it out. A few seconds later we heard, "Oh, my! Well, look at that." He confirmed that there were two innocent babes sound asleep in room number six.

We thought it might be wise to reunite them with their parents, and so we opened our window to let them clamber into our room and through to the sleeping innocents.

The next morning at breakfast we sat down only to burst into laughter when our neighbors joined us at the table. Our giggling proved contagious and soon the entire breakfast room was chuckling as all the guests had heard the parents' peculiar reunion with their children. When we caught our breath we analyzed last night's dinner.

Sharon had never eaten guinea fowl before and simply loved the combination of apple and roasted red beets. Peter had never had a salad like that and pronounced the "saladissimo" the best he had ever eaten.

Later, when checking out to continue our separate ways, Duane parted with the words, "It's like I have always known you."

Guinea Fowl and Red Beets
Serves 4 to 6

- 1 guinea fowl (keep the liver)
- 3 tablespoons olive oil
- Pepper
- Salt
- 3.5 ounces (100 grams) bacon cut into small cubes
- 1 small bunch fresh sage, chopped
- 1 apple, chopped
- 3 cloves garlic, finely chopped
- 3 bay leaves
- 1 small bunch fresh oregano
- 1 teaspoon juniper berries
- 5 bacon rashers
- 300 grams golf-ball-sized red beets
- 1 tablespoon ginger syrup

Rub the guinea fowl with 1 tablespoon olive oil, pepper, and salt.
In a bowl, mix the bacon cubes, chopped liver. Mix in half the sage, apple, and garlic. Season to taste with salt and pepper, and stuff the fowl with the mixture.

Place the fowl in a heavy roasting pan on top of the bay leaves, oregano, juniper berries, and the bacon rashers.

Roast on bottom rack of oven at 350 degrees F. (180 degrees C.) until golden and the juices run clear when the thigh is pierced.

Meanwhile, toss the beets with the remaining olive oil and sage on a large baking sheet. Season with pepper and salt. Roast the beets on top rack of oven for about 35 minutes. Add the remaining apple and the ginger syrup and roast for a further 10 minutes.

Serve the fowl with the beets spooned around them and drizzle pan juices over the bird

Saladissimo

Serves 4 to 6

- *1 bunch lamb's lettuce*
- *1 small oak-leaf lettuce*
- *1 bunch arugula*
- *1 small buttercup lettuce*
- *1 yellow pepper*
- *1 cup French beans*

For the dressing:
- *1 tablespoon balsamic vinegar*
- *2 tablespoons olive oil*
- *2 tablespoons walnut oil*
- *1 small bunch basil, finely chopped*
- *3 tablespoons pine nuts, crushed*

Roast the pepper in the oven until the skin blackens, put in a paper bag to cool, then peel and cut into thin strips. Tear the lettuces into bite-size pieces, wash, and spin dry.

Boil the beans until tender but still crunchy.

Blend the ingredients for the dressing into a paste.

Drop the hot beans into the paste and let cool down. Toss the lettuces with the bean mixture and the yellow pepper strips.

Made in the
USA
Columbia, SC